COPYRIGHT, 1914, BY
CHARLES SCRIBNER'S SONS

Published September, 1914

TO GEORGE ARLISS

ON ACTING

I

WHEN George Henry Lewes collected into an invaluable little book his scattered essays 'On Actors and the Art of Acting' he prefixt a prefatory letter to Anthony Trollope, wherein he dwelt on the ignorance of the fundamental basis of the actor's art wide-spread even among men of culture, who would have held it disgraceful to be as ill-informed about the principles of any of the kindred arts. "I have heard those," he wrote, "for whose opinions in other directions my respect is great, utter judgments on this subject which proved that they had not even a suspicion of what the art of acting really is. Whether they blamed or praised, the grounds which they advanced for praise or blame were often questionable."

In the two score years since Lewes made this sweeping assertion the actor has attracted more and more attention; the theater has again established its importance both in Great Britain and the United States; and the drama has shown many signs that it is likely to recover its lost ground among the peoples that speak English. And yet the general ignorance in regard to the art of acting is not less than it was when Lewes was comparing Edmund Kean with Rachel and recording his first impressions of Salvini. A knowledge of the principles of the art is no more widely diffused now than it was when the staple play of the English stage was a mangled and misleading adaptation from the French.

Of course, the unthinking spectators will always fail to give a thought to the unseen dramatist, and they will always confuse the actor with the character he is personating. They will applaud the lovely heroine, because they sympathize with her sufferings or her sentiments, wholly regardless of the artistic accomplishment of the actress who impersonates her; and they will hiss the unsightly villain, whom they detest for his evil intent, even tho the actor taking the part may be the most skilful of the performers. They would discover nothing absurd in the remark of a certain drummer, once made to a distinguisht comedian: "Mr. Drew, I don't see how you manage to think of so many clever things to say on the stage. I wish I could learn to do that offhand. It would be mighty useful to me in my business."

And not only unthinking spectators

are capable of absurdities of this sort, for a similar ignorance is sometimes revealed even by those who are permitted to write theatrical notices in the newspapers. Whoever has occasion to read many of these reports must have seen more than one passage in which the reviewer credited the actor with the ingenuity which the playwright had bestowed on the character. For example, the account of the first performance of a British farce which appeared in one of the New York papers a few years ago stated that "Miss Blank was excellent; in fact, she did quite the cleverest thing in the play when she was quick-witted enough to arrange the furniture so as to deceive the officers of the law." Blunders as flagrant as this are not common, of course; but that they occur at all is evidence of a disheartening misunderstanding of the art of the stage.

ON ACTING

That gross misconceptions of this sort should actually get into print is evidence also of a general belief that dramatic reviewing is very easy, and that anybody may be trusted to write a theatrical notice, however little he knows about the theater. It may be admitted possibly that a descriptive paragraph or two can be considered quite sufficient for the most of the entertainments offered in our play-houses, — entertainments often satisfactory, each in its own fashion, and yet not demanding serious consideration. But circumstances change when an important new play is produced. Then the task of the dramatic reviewer may be both difficult and delicate, since he has to form an opinion as to the merits of the play itself, which he can know only thru this single performance, and at the same time to judge the actors also as they appear in this half-known piece.

In other words, he can see the play only thru the players, as he can see the performers only thru the piece; and either medium may refract so that he shall get a false image.

Sometimes a play of less than average merit may be saved by superior acting, or even by the surpassing personal appeal of the chief actor or actress. The special vocabulary of the theater recognizes this; and it describes certain characters as "parts that play themselves," and certain plays as "actor-proof," meaning thereby that these parts and these plays are likely to please the public even if they are inadequately performed. The stage-folk also know certain characters as "ungrateful parts," recognizing that even the best acting cannot make them satisfactory to the performer or to the spectator. And the French go further: they speak of a "false good part," a *faux bon rôle*, meaning thereby a part which appears to be prominent and important but which is not as rich as it seems, altho its real poverty is often not revealed even to the actor himself until the actual performance. These are subtleties of the histrionic art which are never suspected by the ordinary playgoer, who comes to the theater in search of unthinking recreation. But they need to be mastered by every critic of the acted drama.

II

PROBABLY the ordinary playgoer would be swift to accept the first of two definitions once proposed by Bronson Howard: "The art of acting is the art of moving, speaking, and appearing on the stage as the character assumed would move, speak, and appear in real life, under the circumstances indicated in the play." As he suggested, this appears to be a reasonable definition; but, as he went on to explain, it is "absolutely and radically false," because it leaves out the one essential word. It ought to read: "The art of acting is the art of *seeming* to move, speak, and appear on the stage as the character assumed moves, speaks, and appears in real life, under the circumstances

8

indicated in the play." And the experienced dramatist commented on this second definition and explained that "the actor's art is to make the people in an audience, some of them a hundred feet or more away, *think* that he is moving, speaking, and appearing like the character assumed; and, in nine cases out of ten, the only way to make them think so is *not* to be doing it; to be doing something else."

And in his helpful discussion of his own calling, 'L'Art et le Comédien,' Coquelin insisted on the same point. You may do what you please in your effort to attain the utmost of realism in scenery and in furniture, the stage will ever remain the stage, and it cannot be the real thing. "You are in the theater," the great French actor declared, "and not in the street or at home. If you put on the stage the action of the street or the home, there will result very much what would happen if you were to put a life-sized statue on top of a column: it would no longer seem to be life-sized."

When the sculptor is modeling a statue for the top of a column or for the pediment of a monumental edifice, to be seen only from below, he proportions it to this lofty height, very differently from the way in which he would deal with the same figure if it had to stand by itself on a low pedestal in an open park. So the actor has to adjust his representation of reality to the large theater, so much larger than the room in which the character is supposed to stand. He has to change his scale, to translate the actual reality into the semblance of reality. He can seem real only by not sticking absolutely to the facts. Lewes quoted from the diary of the French comedian Molé a note to the effect that this actor, one evening, was not satisfied with his work, since he had let himself go and had been "too much the character itself" and no longer the actor playing it: "I was real as I would have been at home; I ought to have been real in another way, in accord with the perspective of the theater." This suggests an explanation of the fact that a lady who has stept from society to the stage may appear almost unladylike as an actress, altho in her own home she might be an accomplisht woman of the world. She cannot *seem* what she really *is* because she does not understand the perspective of the theater.

III

TO get a firm grasp of the principles of the art of acting is at least as difficult as it is to seize those of the art of painting; and the inquirer can find most profit in conference with the actual practitioners of the art. Much of the chatter about painters and painting is futile and foolish; and so is most of the chatter about actors and acting. But we can listen with as much pleasure as profit when the artists themselves are willing to talk about their art, to discuss their own way of working, and to reveal the secrets of the craft. As John La Farge once declared, what the artist "has to say about himself and his art is of the utmost use, and, in fact, is the only authority. All people interested, that is to say, all real students, . . . must make the effort to learn in any direction, whatever it may be, — thru the wording of the teachers," — who are also practitioners of the art.

So we learn best about painting from La Farge himself, and from Fromentin, and from a few other painters who happen also to have the critical faculty and the gift of exposition. And in like manner we can find our profit in what the actors have to say about their own art, — not in formal disquisition, but in suggestive discussion of their fellow-craftsmen. It is true that one actor, — Samson, — who was Rachel's trainer, a most finisht comedian, prepared a set treatise on the histrionic art; but his didactic poem, on the model of Horace's 'Art of Poetry,' has never been rendered into English. But we have the incomparable 'Apology for

the Life of Colley Cibber,' and the il-
luminating 'Autobiography' of Joseph
Jefferson, and the stimulating lecture
on the art of the actor by Coquelin,
the most accomplisht of comedians in
the final years of the nineteenth century. And then there is the little col-
lection of essays by George Henry
Lewes, an actor himself, a playwright
also, and the son of an actor, with an
inherited insight into the practise of
the profession.

These are more useful than the works
of the profest critics of the theater,
altho there is much to be gleaned here
and there in the writings of Lamb and
Hazlitt, in the two solid tomes devoted
to the chief figures of the contemporary
French stage by the late Francisque
Sarcey, and in the ingenious inquiry
of Mr. William Archer, which he called
'Masks or Faces,' and in which he collected the evidence for and against

Diderot's 'Paradox' — that the actor must not feel too acutely the emotion he is depicting. Not to be overlookt are the pregnant words of the playwrights also: Shakspere's advice to the Players in 'Hamlet,' Molière's counsel to his own comrades in the 'Impromptu of Versailles,' and Legouvé's excellent papers on Rachel and Ristori. The relation of the dramaturgic art to the histrionic must ever be very close; and the dramatist has perforce to acquire a certain knowledge of the actors' technic, or else he will not be able properly to prepare what he is devising for their use.

IV

THE dramatic poet always intends his works for the stage itself; he plans them to be performed before an audience, in a theater, and by actors. Therefore he is ever taking account of the spectators, and of their prejudices and of their predilections; he is always careful to adjust his work to the actual conditions of the theater of his own time; and he utilizes to the utmost the special qualifications of the actors who take part in the performance. A great poet cannot write a play without considering the actor's art, any more than he can write a lyric to be set to music without considering the vocalist's art. Shelley is a far finer lyrist than Moore, but the Irish bard sang his songs into being, and their open vowels are ever a delight to the singer; whereas the English poet, giving little thought to the musician, filled his lyrics with consonants which close the mouth. "The stage is to the prose-drama," so Mr. Henry James once remarkt, "what the time is to the song, or the concrete case to the general law."

It is at his peril that the playwright does not take the player into account. No one of the great dramatists, it is well to remember, has ever failed to maintain cordial relations with the several performers of his plays. Better than any one else, the great dramatist knew how much he might be indebted to the actors, to their skill, to their sympathy, and to their loyalty. Sometimes, it is true, we find an author who has sought success on the stage without attaining the aim of his

V

HE acts with his own person, and that must ever be the material of his art. He is fortunate, indeed, if he happens to be young and handsome, strong of limb and manly in bearing, with expressive eyes and a moving voice. These natural gifts will carry him along, if only he can acquire even a slight acquaintance with the elements of his art. Many a pretty woman has gone on the stage and won immediate popularity by her personal charm alone, by the compelling power of her youth, her grace, and her beauty. This is what Fanny Kemble did; and yet she admitted at once the justice of Macready's assertion that she did not know the rudiments of her profession.

Descended from a race of artists, the daughter of Charles Kemble recognized that she herself was only an amateur. Another lady who had met with a similar success for similar reasons, but who married and gave up the theater after two or three years of acting, once confest to me, later in life, that it was only toward the end of her brief career on the stage that she had begun to find out how she made her effects, learning doubtfully how to control them and how to repeat them night after night. That is to say, the actress was just learning the rudiments of her profession, altho the woman had long won by her personal attraction a prosperous popularity in the theater.

This it is that chiefly distinguishes the actors from all other artists, — that they must do their work with their own persons and in public. The poet may retire to an ivory tower far away, and the painter may prefer a remote solitude; they separate what they do from themselves, and they send this away. They are not present when we read the poem or see the picture. They do not come into direct contact with us, and they may ignore us, if they see fit. But the actor must work in the presence of the public, and the material of his art is himself. And this again accounts for the acuter sensitiveness of the actor to criticism. It is easy enough to discuss what the poet has done, or the painter, without personal comment. But how is it possible to separate the art of the actor from his personality? How can the artist and the man be disentangled? How may an adverse criticism on the performance of a part avoid the appearance of an adverse criticism on the personal characteristics of the human being who has put himself inside the character? Perhaps it might be achieved by a critic of extraordinary skill and delicacy; but it is too much to expect from the average theatrical reviewer.

It was a wise appreciation of this fact which led Edwin Booth to recommend the permanent debarring of the profest theatrical reviewer from membership in The Players, the club which he founded for his own profession and for the practitioners of the allied arts of literature, painting, sculpture, architecture, and music. Even the journalist, as such, is not excluded, so long as he will refrain from the discussion of contemporary actors. The literary critic is admitted, since any author must be strangely thin-skinned who cannot sit at meat with the writer of an adverse review; and the critic of painting is made welcome, since the painter and his work are easily separable. But the histrionic critic must remain outside the doors of The Players since he cannot, whatever his good will, deal with the actor without lapsing into personal comment on the man. This rule of The Players is an unwritten law only, but it is always obeyed; and more than one member attracted to theatrical reviewing has had reluctantly to renounce the privilege of being a Player. This wise rule has only one disadvantage: by keeping the actor and the critic apart it lessens the opportunity of the latter to learn more about the art of the former.

VI

TO win a fair proportion of popular approval an actor needs only an attractive personality and also a modicum of the mimetic faculty, — of the special aptitude for the stage, which is as distinct a gift as the aptitude for story-telling, or for making verses, or for acquiring money. The successful actor may happen also to be a man of wide intelligence, as Garrick was, and Coquelin also; but he is no more likely to have an acute intellect than is a successful novelist or a successful business man. The men who make money and the men who write popular novels may or may not be possest of remarkable mental ability; they have succeeded rather by virtue of their special aptitude for story-telling or for money-making. The special aptitude of the actor may be accompanied by ability in other directions; but the possession of the special aptitude is not evidence that he has also the wider intelligence.

Just as Paul Morphy was the foremost of chess-players, but in other respects only a man of ordinary capacity, so an actor of high rank may be no more brilliant than the average man. Mrs. Siddons was the greatest of *Lady Macbeths*, with an incomparable skill in sounding the unseen depths of that tragic figure; but the essay she wrote on the subject is almost valueless. Salvini was the greatest of *Othellos*, with a lofty largeness of imaginative interpretation; but his critical papers on the part do not display any special insight. Mrs. Siddons and Salvini were dowered with the special aptitude of acting, and they cultivated this gift loyally and diligently; but outside of their acting they were only ordinary mortals.

Probably this is what Lewes had in mind when he asserted that "people generally overrate a fine actor's genius, and underrate his trained skill. They are apt to credit him with a power of intellectual conception and poetic creation to which he has really a very slight claim, and fail to recognize all the difficulties which his artistic training has enabled him to master." What the actor must have, if he is to rise high in his art, is not general intelligence but the special intelligence of his own art, the intuitive understanding of its possibilities and of its limitations, the clear insight into its principles and the power swiftly to apply them. That he should always be conscious of the full effect of what he does, that he should always know just why he does it, — this is not at all necessary, for often the best work of the artist is instinctive. He does what he does because that is indeed the only way for him to do it. There is no need that he should be conscious of his processes, or that he should be able to trace the steps that led him to the satisfactory result. Poe is not a greater poet because he has analized the succession of motives which had led him to the composition of the 'Raven.'

Like all other artists, the actor is greatest in his achievement when he has builded better than he knew. His native aptitude and his artistic training enable him to produce an impression which often seems to be the result of pure intellectual power. Planché has an anecdote in point: The day after the first performance of a play of his in which a certain comedian had given an intelligent and impressive performance of a leading character, this actor applied to the author for the loan of the manuscript, explaining that he had been absent when the play had been read to the company and he did not really "know what it was all about." And yet, his innate gift and his skill in his own calling had permitted him to profit by the hints of the stage-manager at rehearsal, and so to deliver the words of his part as to suggest a keen intellectual appreciation of the action, even if he did not "know what it was all about." He had not had wit enough to find out the story of the play before he acted in it; and yet when he acted it he seemed to display ample intelligence.

VII

IN one of M. Jean Richepin's stories
of stage-life, there is a veracious
portrait of a broken-down actor so
enamored of his art that he must ever
be teaching it, wherefore he has gath-
ered about him a group of ambitious
urchins whom he instructs in acting and
to whom he imparts the principles of
the craft. He has the actor's frequent
contempt for the mere author of the
play, and he impresses on his young
pupils that they are always to go behind the words of their parts to the
emotions evoked by the situation itself, since it is the duty of the actor to
express these emotions richly and com-
pletely, no matter how poorly and
meagerly the author may have voiced

them. Even if the words happen to be inadequate or halting, the actor must take care to convey the sentiment fully to the audience. And then, to emphasize the unimportance of the mere word, the old instructor picked out a common phrase — indeed, one of the vulgarest of all — and bade his little pupils repeat that single phrase with the feeling proper to each of a series of situations, — making love to a lady, defying a rival, blessing a child, and saying farewell to a dying mother. He made them employ always this same vulgar phrase, surcharging it with the full emotion belonging to each of these several actions.

Altho there is more than a hint of caricature in M. Richepin's sketch, the method of his old comedian is praiseworthy; it is by such emotional gymnastic as this that the performer acquires flexibility. The actor needs to have under control not only his gestures and his tones, but all other means of simulating sensibility; and these should be ready for use at all times, wholly independent of the words of the text. He must be able so to breathe, "Mesopotamia," that it shall seem to be a blessed word, indeed. He must be ready to rival the feat credited to Madame Modjeska at a reception in New York, when she was askt to recite in Polish. For a while she demurred, but at last she yielded to the urging of her friends. Standing at one end of the room, she began to repeat a strangely rhythmic composition, unintelligible of course to her hearers, altho they could catch the occurrence of the same sounds at intervals. At first it seemed simple enough, apparently with some give and take of question and answer; and then it became pathetic, and as she spoke the saddening words the voice of the accomplisht actress broke. There was almost a sob in her tones, and there were tears ready to fall from her eyes. But her husband, Count Bozenta, the one person in the company who understood Polish, had to leave the room to restrain his laughter, because what she was delivering thus emotionally was only the multiplication-table!

Here the actress was feigning a succession of moods and a variety of emotions without any support of helpful suggestion from the empty words which fell from her lips. Her feat was akin to the primitive communication of feeling without the aid of language. The syllables she uttered were meaningless or contradictory, but they served as the medium to carry the emotion she desired to convey. The Italian tragedian Ernesto Rossi used to assert that "a great actor is independent of the poet, because the supreme essence of feeling does not reside in prose or in verse, but in the accent with which it is delivered."

This is not a specimen of professional vainglory, altho it may have that appearance. It is only the overstatement of a fact. It is supported by the anecdote of Madame Modjeska; and Rossi himself used to adduce as evidence in its behalf a little story even more striking. He was having supper one evening at Padua with half-a-dozen fellow-actors, and they fell into discussion of their own art and of its possibilities. One of them pickt up the bill of fare and declared his intention of reading this barren list so pathetically as to bring tears to their eyes. The other actors refused to believe that this was possible; they were not credulous spectators; they were hardened to every trick of the trade; and they smiled at his proposal. The first words he read simply, rising soon to a large dignity of utterance that veiled the commonplace syllables. Then his rich, full voice began to tremble as if with fear, and to quiver at length as tho the soul of the speaker was pierced with poignant agony. Despite the repugnant words, which ceased to be perceived clearly, the sweeping emotions with which his tones were charged proved to be irresistibly contagious; and long before he had read to the end of the bill of fare, his comrades found themselves looking at each other with tears rolling down their cheeks.

The feat of the Italian actor is even stranger and less credible than that of the Polish actress. She had the advantage of an unknown tongue, and she had to move only sympathetic and responsive hearers, whereas he was able to conquer expert witnesses who understood the meaning of every syllable of the incongruous text he was reading. Moreover, the friends of Madame Modjeska were taken unawares, whereas Rossi and the other actors had hardened their hearts to resist, and must have been taken captive in spite of their resistance.

VIII

THE French author of the pleasant book about the contemporary Italian stage from which this little story has been borrowed, failed to record the name of the actor who was the hero of Rossi's anecdote, and who, very likely, was not a performer of high rank. Even if he had at his command the perfect control of a beautiful voice, he may have been devoid of other necessary implements of his art. Above all, he may have lacked that "intelligence of his profession" which alone would enable him to employ these implements to best advantage. The mere possession of all the tools of his trade does not of itself make the craftsman. The means of expression, however ample and however varied, are useless unless there is something to express, — and something which it is worth while to express.

Many an actor strong in execution is weak in conception. He does not know what it is best for him to do, tho he knows how to do it when this is shown to him. He needs guidance and he cannot steer himself, altho he is certain to make a swift trip if only his course is directed by a wiser head. Here is the duty and the opportunity of the dramatist himself, or of the producer of the play, who need not be much of an actor, but who must know how the play ought to be acted in every part, and who can suggest to the several performers the various effects they are to accomplish. It may sound like a paradox to assert that the author of a play, who often cannot act at all, can yet teach the actors who are his masters in this art; but this is exactly what he may have to do. Sardou has told us that he schooled Anaïs Fargueil in many of the effects he had studied in Ristori's acting.

Sometimes, it is true, the playwright may be also an accomplisht actor, and the result of this combination is generally very advantageous. A play of Mr. Gillette's or of the late James A. Herne's, in which the author himself acted, appeared always to be performed by comedians of unusual intelligence. Sometimes the manager of the theater, or the stage-manager who brings out plays, has this power of suggesting and controlling and guiding. Sometimes even performers of the highest distinction have been indebted to a teacher who lighted the path that else they would have trodden in darkness. This dependence of the performer on the trainer has been excellently seized by Thackeray in 'Pendennis,' wherein we are shown how Little Bowes the fiddler had taught the lovely Miss Fotheringay, — how he was the organist and how she was the instrument whose music has been evoked by him, hidden and unsuspected.

Finer actresses by far than the adored Miss Fotheringay have owed much to a trainer in the background. Even the great Mrs. Siddons was indebted for many of her effects to the inventive brain of her brother, John Philip Kemble. The great Rachel, again, was the pupil of Samson, a little comic actor, who yet was able to teach her how to attain to the loftiest heights of tragedy. She used to say that she was "lame on one side" until Samson had shown her what to do with a part. Legouvé has recorded how she turned to Samson during one of the rehearsals of 'Adrienne Lecouvreur' and, in the presence of her assembled comrades, exprest her gratitude to him, who had shown her how to get the best out of herself.

Every one at all familiar with the inner history of the stage in Great Britain and the United States during the last quarter of the nineteenth century is aware that two of the actresses who have held a foremost position in the theater of both countries were immensely indebted to the constant counsel of two of their professional associates. They had each of them, not exactly a Little Bowes in the background, but a Samson, who guided them and who trained them to get the utmost out of their histrionic gift. To the unthinking spectators in the theaters of London and New York the performances of these charming actresses appeared to be singularly spontaneous and freely individual. Yet this free spontaneity was the result of their being able to take a hint, to assimilate the suggestion they received, and to profit by it, each in her own fashion and in accord with her own temperament. Each of them was an emotional instrument, played on by a far keener artistic intelligence than her own.

IX

WHEN the keen artistic intelligence and the rich emotional instrument happen to be in the possession of the same person, then the world is likely to have another great actor. The intelligence alone will not suffice, or else Shakspere would have been the foremost actor of his day, and not Burbage. The emotion alone will not do it, unless it can express itself adequately by voice and look and gesture, — "the actor's symbols," as Lewes calls them, thru which he makes intelligible the emotions of the character he is personating. "No amount of sensibility will avail unless it can express itself adequately by these symbols. It is not enough for an actor to *feel:* he must *represent.* He must express his feelings in symbols universally intelligible and affecting."

If we may rely on the testimony of Lewes himself, actors as prominent as Macready and Charles Kean, men of intelligence and of character both of them, did not really attain to the highest altitudes of their art, because of their defective control of these symbols, the result of purely physical disadvantages. As we study the long annals of the theater, striving to ascertain what player most certainly combined in himself all the attributes of a truly great actor, we are likely to be led to the conclusion that no one has a better claim to the supreme chieftainship of the histrionic art than David Garrick, equally powerful in comedy and in tragedy, and as warmly welcomed in France as he was highly esteemed in England:

ON ACTING

As an actor, confest without rival to shine:
As a wit, if not first, in the very first line.

In our own day we have been fortunate in the privilege of studying two of the masters of the stage, — Jefferson and Coquelin, — probably as accomplisht and as richly endowed as any of their predecessors in the theater, gifted by nature and trained by art. Having something within them to express, and possessing perfect command of the symbols of expression, they had also, each of them, wide cultivation, unusual intelligence, and delightful individuality.

X

DAVID GARRICK may have been the greatest actor the world has ever seen; but what is he to-day but a faint memory — a name in the biographical dictionaries, and little more? Joseph Jefferson was the most delightful comedian of the English-speaking stage at the end of the nineteenth century; but his fame will fade like Garrick's, and in a score of years he also will be but a name, and no longer an alert personality sharp in the recollection of all living playgoers. This swift removal to the limbo of the vanisht is the fate of all actors, however popular in their own day, and however indisputable their manifold gifts.

And this fate the actor shares with all performers, — orators, vocalists, and instrumentalists. It is a fate from which the practitioners of the other arts are preserved by the fact that their works may live after them, whereas the performers can leave nothing behind them but the splendid recollection that may linger in the memories of those who beheld the performance. Goldsmith was the friend of Garrick; and there are thousands today who have enjoyed the quaint simplicity of the 'Vicar of Wakefield,' and to whom therefore Goldsmith is something more than a mere name. Macready was the friend of Bulwer-Lytton, who wrote for him the 'Lady of Lyons' and 'Richelieu'; but the actor left the stage more than half a century ago and has been forgotten by the play-goers, who long continued to attend the countless performances of the two plays Macready had originally produced.

The actors are moved often to repeat the pathetic query of *Rip* when he returned from his sleep of twenty years, "Are we, then, so soon forgot?" And Jefferson himself answered the question in the affirmative. He told Mr. Francis Wilson that Betterton and Garrick, Kean and Mrs. Siddons, "mark milestones in the dramatic pathway, for they lived at a time when literary men wrote sympathetically of the stage, and so their memories are kept alive." He thought that Edwin Booth might be more than a tradition solely because he had founded a club — The Players — whereby his fame would be kept green. When Mr. Wilson then askt him about himself, the shrewd comedian explained that his own 'Autobiography' might serve to rescue him from total oblivion. And he summed up the case and dismist it finally with the assertion that "the painter, the sculptor, the author, all live in their works after death, — but there is nothing so useless as a dead actor! Acting is a tradition. Actors must have their reward now, in the applause of the public, — or never. If their names live, it must be because of some extraneous circumstance."

Other distinguisht actors have phrased the same thought even more forcibly. Delaunay, for a third of a century the ideal young lover in all the masterpieces of dramatic literature performed at the Théâtre Français, used to liken the actor to the painter in Hoffmann's weird tale, who sat before a blank canvas with an empty brush and yet gave all the touches needed for a true picture. And Lawrence Barrett was fond of repeating an anecdote of Michelangelo. To please some exacting patron or to gratify a whim of his own, the great artist, so it is said, once carved a statue of snow. This may have been the final expression of his plastic genius; but it endured only until the sun shone again. Then it melted swiftly into a shapeless lump, and soon it was gone forever, leaving no record of its powerful beauty. "And this is what the actor does every night," so Barrett was wont to comment; "he is forever carving a statue of snow."

XI

SO strong is the instinctive human desire for immortality, so abiding is the wish of man to transmit to those who may come after some testimony of himself, that these regretful utterances of the actors are very natural, indeed. But is their case really as hard as they think it? Has the actor no compensation for the transitoriness of his fame?

And when we seek an honest answer to these questions, we can find one without difficulty. Indeed, we can find two, — one of them obvious enough, and the other perhaps not so evident, but not less suggestive.

The first answer is contained in Jefferson's assertion that "actors must have their reward now, in the applause of the public, — or never." And we all know that actors do have their reward, — an ample reward, prest down and running over. Both in praise and in cash, the actor is better paid than any other artist. In proportion to his accomplishment, he is greatly overpaid, since the nightly salary of a prima donna far overtops the modest fee of the composer of the opera. The possible earnings of celebrated performers are almost fabulous, now that they can make the whole world tributary. It may be that the pecuniary gains of a very popular actor are not actually greater than those of a very popular novelist or of a very popular portrait-painter. But where there are today only one or two novelists and portrait-painters who have attained to this summit of prosperity, there are a dozen or a score of actors and of actresses

who are reaping the richest of harvests.
And even the rank and file of the histrionic profession are better paid than
are the average practitioners of the
other arts.

The actor, overpaid in actual money
so far as his real ability is concerned,
is also unduly rewarded with adula-
tion. In the general ignorance about
the art of acting, he is often rated far
more highly than he deserves. He is
greeted with public acclaim; and he
can rejoice in the wide reverberations
of a notoriety which is the immediate
equivalent of fame. He comes almost
in personal contact with his admirers,
and they are loud in expressing to him
the pleasure he has just given them.
Far more directly and far more keenly
than any poet or any sculptor can the
actor breathe up the incense that is
offered to him. And if he happen to
be a Kemble, he may have the good

fortune to listen while a Campbell declares acting to be the supreme art:

> For ill can Poetry express
>   Full many a tone of thought sublime,
> And painting, mute and motionless,
>   Steals but a glance of Time.
> But by the mighty actor brought,
>   Illusion's perfect triumphs come, —
> Verse ceases to be airy thought,
>   And Sculpture to be dumb.

Even if the actor is not a Kemble and does not receive the homage of a Campbell, even if he is but one of the many stars that twinkle in the theatrical firmament, he has a celebrity denied to other artists. He may expect to be recognized as he passes in the street. He may count on the public familiarity with his name, such as no other artist could hope for. Few of those who throng thru the portals of a noble building ever give a thought to the architect whose work it is. Few of those who stand in admiration before a stately statue in a public square ever ask the name of the sculptor who wrought it.

Even in the theater itself only a few of those who sit entranced at the performance of a play know or care to know its authorship. Bronson Howard was once askt how many of the audience that filled the theater at the hundredth performance of one of his plays would be aware that he was the author of the piece they were enjoying; and he answered that he doubted if one in ten of the spectators happened to be acquainted with his name. But at least nine in ten of the spectators knew the names of the stars; and when that piece chanced to be performed later by one of the stock-companies, it was advertised as "Robson and Crane's great play, the 'Henrietta.'" So it is that the player is ever overshadowing the playwright, altho the actor is but the interpreter of what the author has created. It is the incalculable advantage of the actor that "he stands in the suffused light of emotion kindled by the author," so Lewes declared, adding that the performer delivering "the great thoughts of an impassioned mind, is rewarded as the bearer of glad tidings is rewarded, tho he may have had nothing to do with the facts which he narrates."

XII

A CERTAIN rough-and-ready justice there is in most of the affairs
of this life; and by this those who have
their brief hour upon the stage may
profit, like the rest of us. The obvious
compensation for the swift forgetting
that may follow the most renowned
actor's withdrawal from active service
in the theater, is to be found in the fact
that while he was prominent before
the footlights he was probably more or
less overpaid either in approbation or
in money, and possibly in both. But
there is another compensation less obvious, and indeed wholly overlookt
by those who have discust the subject.
Even Lewes failed to state it, altho
he seems to have been almost in sight
of it.

"It is thought a hardship that great actors in quitting the stage can leave no monument more solid than a name," so Lewes wrote commenting on the retirement of Macready. "The painter leaves behind him pictures to attest his power; the author leaves behind him books; the actor leaves only a tradition. The curtain falls — the artist is annihilated. Succeeding generations may be told of his genius; none can test it." But Lewes did not see the significance of these final words: "none can test it." They suggest that in one respect, at least, the actor may be more fortunate than any other artist. His fame in the future depends absolutely on the reputation which he achieved while he was alive and active in his profession. From that pedestal he can never be deposed. On that height he is secure, whatever the changes of critical theory and whatever the vagaries of public opinion. For him the judgment of his contemporaries is final; and posterity has no court of appeal. The election on the face of the returns must stand; and it can never be voided later, since the ballots have been destroyed.

This is a security of tenure possest by no painter and by no poet, whose works survive to be valued anew by the changing standards of successive generations. Painters exalted in one century as indisputable masters have been cast down in another century and denounced as mere pretenders. Pope was acclaimed in his own day as the greatest of English poets, only to be disdained in a few score years as an adroit versifier, a mere wit, not fairly to be termed a poet at all. From these vicissitudes of criticism the actor is preserved; his fame cannot be impeacht. No critic can move for a retrial of Garrick; the witnesses are all dead; the case is closed; the decision stands forever. "Succeeding generations may be told of his genius; none can test it;" — and because none can test it, succeeding generations must accept what they have been told. Garrick painted his picture with an empty brush, it is true, and he had to carve his statue in the snow; and therefore neither the picture nor the statue can ever be seen again by unfriendly eyes. The skill of the artist cannot be proved; we have to take it on trust and to hold it as a matter of faith.

Beyond all question, it may be a signal advantage to the actor that he can leave behind him nothing whereby his contemporary fame may be contested by those who come after him. How great an advantage it may be, we may gage by considering the sadly shrunken reputations today of certain speakers accepted in their own time as orators of compelling force. In the eighteenth century, Whitefield was a widely popular preacher, credited with genuine eloquence by all who heard him. One discourse of his was so moving that it coaxed the copper and the silver and the gold out of the pockets of the calm and unemotional Franklin. If we had only the testimony of those who heard him gladly, we could hardly fail to regard Whitefield as one of the really great orators of the world. Unfortunately for the fame of the fervid preacher, some of his sermons survive to bear witness against him. Whitefield's burning words, powerfully effective as they were when sustained by his artful delivery, are cold enough now that we have them on the printed page.

What happened to Whitefield in the

eighteenth century is not unlike what happened to Gladstone in the nineteenth. There would be little possibility of denying to the great party-leader a foremost place among the world's mightiest orators, if we had only the record of the overwhelming effect produced upon those whom he addressed, whether he was carrying the fiery cross thru Midlothian or holding the house entranced hour after hour by a speech on the budget. Not Webster, not Cicero, not Demosthenes was more powerful in producing results. But we are not compelled to rely solely on the recollections of those who sat silent under the spell of his commanding personality. When we seek to test Gladstone's title to be held a great orator, we can call other witnesses, — these very speeches themselves, revised by the speaker himself; and they bear testimony against him,

just as Whitefield's sermons bear testimony against Whitefield.

The reputation of Gladstone and of
Whitefield as orators would be higher
than it is, if they were judged only by
the memories of those who heard them,
or by the record made by those who
were still under the spell of their in-
fluence. Herein the actors are luckier
than the orators, since it is by the en-
thusiastic record alone that they can
be judged. There can be no other
proof of their great gifts; and "none
can test it."

XIII

IT is true that now and again a skeptic stands up to suggest a doubt whether the renowned actors of the past really deserved their reputations. He wonders how they would be received today, and whether we should esteem Burbage and Betterton and Edmund Kean as highly as they were once esteemed, each in his own day. He even ventures to opine that if these great actors could appear on our stage today, we should find them old-fashioned, of course, and probably also stilted and stagy. And altho this suggestion is disconcerting, it contains a certain measure of truth. The acting of the past was not exactly like the acting of the present, because the circumstances of performance have been continually changing, even if the principles of the art abide unaltered.

The actor must ever adjust himself to the theater in which he is performing. His methods must be modified in accordance with the condition of the stage at the time. Burbage played his parts on a bare platform thrust out into the unroofed yard; and Edmund Kean won his triumphs in a huge theater with the oil-footlights curving out far beyond the curtain. Burbage and Kean had to accept these conditions and to adjust their technic accordingly. If they were to appear today in the modern playhouse with its picture-frame stage, and if they were to act as they were wont to act in the wholly different playhouse of the platform-stage type, no doubt they would disappoint us, and we might very well fail to perceive their real merits. But this is not the fair way to put it. If Garrick were to be born again, and to grow up amid our conditions, he would accept these and find his profit in them. His histrionic genius would expand as freely now as it did then; and he would be as responsive to the pressure of public expectation in the twentieth century as he was in the eighteenth.

XIV

THERE are certain parrot-cries that are forever echoing down the corridor of Time. Every young generation hears them, and is forced to wonder how much truth they may contain. Perhaps the most insistent of these immortal complaints is that which keeps on declaring the decline of the drama. That the theater is going to the dogs, — this is what we may hear on every hand. But a little knowledge of the last century is reassuring, since we learn then that our fathers and our grandfathers, and the grandfathers of our grandfathers, were all of them told that the stage had fallen on evil days and that its future would certainly be inferior to its past. Sometimes it is the organization of the theater which is said to be at fault; sometimes it is dearth of good actors; and sometimes it is the scarcity of good plays and the steady deterioration of the art of the dramatist.

When Colley Cibber asked Congreve why he did not write another comedy, the old wit retorted promptly, "But where are your actors?" And Colley Cibber was one of a group of actors and actresses as brilliant and as accomplisht as ever graced the stage in Great Britain. Sir Philip Sidney almost wept over the pitiful condition of the English drama, just before Shakspere came forward with his swift succession of masterpieces. If we go back many centuries to Greece, we find Aristophanes lamenting the decay of dramatic literature as evidenced in the plays of Euripides. And when Thespis first started out with his cart, — the ear-

liest recorded attempt of any star-
actor to go on the road with his own
company, — we may be certain that
there were not lacking veteran play-
goers who promptly foresaw the speedy
decline of the drama.

Just now, at the beginning of the
twentieth century, when our theaters
are more beautiful and more artistically adorned than ever before, and
when scenery and costumes and all
needful accessories are more carefully
considered, attention is loudly called
to the feebleness of the average play
and to the inefficiency of the average
actor. And yet a moment's reflection
ought to make it plain that there never
has been any period when the average
play and the average actor deserved
unfailing praise. Even in the greatest
epochs of the drama the average play
was none too good. We are all familiar with the comedies of Sheridan

and Goldsmith; but we do not recall the forgotten efforts of Cumberland and Kelly, who shared the stage with them. We point with pride to Shakspere; but we do not pine for a revival of the pieces of Dekker and Heywood. We know that Corneille and Molière and Racine were the masters of the French theater under Louis XIV; but most of us are absolutely ignorant even of the faded names of their contemporary rivals.

Obviously it is unfair to crush the average playmaker of today by a comparison with the greatest dramatists of other days. And every one who has studied the recent history of the theater will admit, if he is both competent and candid, that the outlook for the future is far more hopeful than it was forty or fifty years ago. The technic of the dramaturgic art is far better understood now than it was a little while ago; and in every modern language there are men of ability who have mastered this technic and who are striving to set on the stage the themes, the manners, and the characters of this new century. Ibsen and Björnson are dead; but Hervieu and Brieux, Rostand and Lavedan, are writing in France, as Sudermann and Hauptmann are in Germany and d'Annunzio in Italy. In England there are Sir James Barrie and Mr. Shaw, Mr. Jones and Sir Arthur Pinero; and here in America there are half-a-dozen men, still young most of them, and still learning how to see the life about them and how to reproduce it on the stage, who are earnestly seeking as best they can to hold the mirror up to nature.

If the theaters are beyond all dispute better than they were a few years ago, and if the dramatic literature of the present bids fair to be more satisfactory in the future, the sole remaining point of attack is the acting. What is the profit in a rebirth of dramatic literature if there are no performers to embody it? Where are your actors? Where are the Booths, the Kembles, the Garricks of our time? Where is even that much vaunted old-fashioned stock-company, capable of presenting the old comedies because every member was a trained artist? With our syndicates and our star-system, and our long runs, the art of acting is doomed without hope of recovery. Who shall be bold enough to controvert prophecies of evil?

It calls for little hardihood to deny this and for little knowledge of the theater to disprove it. The Booths and the Kembles and the Garricks did not all live at once; and it is absurd to suppose that we can match all the mighty actors of the past in a single quarter of a century. We may even admit that the English-speaking stage happens for the moment to be without any histrionic artists of the acknowledged eminence of Irving and Jefferson and Booth. But to say this is not to admit that we are poverty-stricken, and that our theater is devoid of many players of admirable accomplishment both in Great Britain and the United States. We all know better. We can easily call the roll of a dozen or a score of actors who are artists, gifted by nature and cultivated by long exercise of their powers, possessing each of them an individuality of his own. Indeed, the list of these performers of high merit is so long that it would be invidious to attempt to set it down here. We can each of us make it up to suit our own likings.

XV

AND yet in fairness the admission must be made, not only that our stage just now happens to lack any performers of the acknowledged preëminence of Booth and Irving and Jefferson, but also that there is a fair foundation for the assertion that we do not now see the old comedies as well acted as they were a few years ago at Daly's, a little earlier at Wallack's, and still further back at the Haymarket in London. This admission can be made frankly and without also admitting that it implies any necessary degeneracy of the art of acting. The so-called "old comedies" — the 'School for Scandal' and the 'Rivals,' 'She Stoops to Conquer' and 'London Assurance' and 'Money' — were written for a theater in which the conditions were very different from those which obtain in the playhouses of this twentieth century, and they called for acting different in kind from the acting appropriate on our modern stage.

Sheridan and Goldsmith and Boucicault wrote for a theater which was so insufficiently lighted, either with oil or gas, that the stage had to curve far out into the auditorium, to form what was known as the "apron"; and on this apron, in the full glare of the footlights, the actor came forward, far in front of the proscenium-arch in which the curtain rose and fell. In our modern playhouses, every part of the stage is adequately illuminated by the electric light, and the apron has disappeared, so that the actor now does his work behind the proscenium-arch and remote from the audience. Half a century ago the actor was really performing on a platform thrust out into the audience, whereas today he is removed behind a picture-frame. The so-called "old comedies" were written for the platform-stage, and they had the oratorical manner proper enough on a platform. Our modern plays are written for the picture-frame stage, and their dialog is far less rhetorical, far simpler, far more "natural" than was appropriate to the theater of the last generation.

It is no wonder, therefore, that the actors of our time, accustomed to these more natural modern pieces, have not preserved the artificial tradition establisht long ago for the proper performance of plays written to suit the very different conditions of an earlier theater that has now ceased to be. The best acting today is adjusted to the stage of today; and the best actors are striving for veracity of character-delineation of a kind almost impossible on the stage of yesterday. Their methods are necessarily different from the methods of their predecessors in the playhouses of half a century ago; but even if different, these methods are not necessarily artistically inferior. Ristori, for example, was reckoned a fine actress in her time, yet she would seem strangely old-fashioned, and perhaps even stagy, to us who are familiar with the simpler and profounder art of Duse. Ristori was a mistress of all the histrionic devices which belonged to the platform-stage, whereas Duse has adjusted her art to the later conditions of the picture-frame theater.

Probably very few of those who are studying the stage have yet seized the full significance of this change in the relation of the actor to the audience,

— this withdrawal of the performer from the platform almost surrounded by the spectators behind a frame which sets him apart and keeps him remote. This modification of the circumstances of performance, like all other modifications that have preceded it in the long evolution of the theater, has had its effect on the dramatist as well as on the comedian. Duse is not more different from Ristori than is the 'Cavalleria Rusticana,' in which she appears, different in its method from the 'Marie Antoinette,' in which the earlier Italian actress was so successful half a century ago. Of course, this change in the aims of the playwrights is not to be ascribed solely to the modification of theatrical conditions, for it is coincident also with the spread of realism. If Ibsen strove to present human nature as he saw it, with the utmost simplicity and directness, and if he es-

chewed rhetorical amplifications accept-
able enough to our grandfathers, there
is a double explanation. His attitude
is partly the result of that wide-spread
movement in favor of a bolder veracity than literature had aimed at
before Balzac set the example; and it
is also partly the result of the new opportunity proffered by the picture-
frame of the modern theater, which
seems to demand a more accurate re-
production of the characteristic background and a closer relation of character to environment.

There is no need of insisting that
the more modern methods of the drama
are better than the older. Indeed, the
more we consider the conditions of the
Greek theater and of the Elizabethan
theater, the more clearly can we perceive that they also had advantages
of their own not to be found in the
theater of our time. But it is for the

theater of our time that our dramatists must compose their plays; and it is in the theater of our time that our actors must act. The theater of the Greeks cannot be resuscitated today any more than the theater of the Elizabethans. And it is with the theater of today, and not with the theater of any yesterday, that both playwright and performer have to deal. Those who have the pleasant privilege of advancing years, and who can therefore look back to earlier conditions, may not like the conditions that obtain now. And there is no cause for wonder in the fact that some of them think that the change is for the worse.

XVI

IT will surprise no one to learn that Joseph Jefferson found it difficult to reconcile himself to the newer practises. He was himself an actor who sought truth as he saw it; but he did not relish the larger proportion of actual fact that he found presented in certain recent plays. I can recall a conversation with him during Duse's first visit to the United States, not long after he had seen her performance in 'Cavalleria Rusticana.' "It's too realistic," he said to me; "altogether too realistic. Why, I could count all the fleas in that Italian village!"

And here is the difficulty of the modern school of actors. They are seeking to present character as sincerely as

they can; they have relinquisht many
of the effects which actors of an earlier
generation delighted in; and as a result they may sometimes seem tame
and pale to those who are looking for
the kind of acting which was appropriate enough in plays of a more florid
type. It is this which underlies the
accusation brought against one very
modern actress, — that "she overacts
her underacting." It is this which
underlay the complaint of the old
actor in Sir Arthur Pinero's delightful
'Trelawney of the Wells,' — that the
part given to him in the new play
had n't a single speech in it, — not
what you could call a speech, — not
a speech that you could "sink your
teeth in"!

We need not be astonisht that actors who overact their underacting
should seem out of place and ill at ease
in the older plays which abound in

speeches that you can sink your teeth in. This is the chief reason why many recent revivals of old plays have seemed to us unsatisfactory. The actor was called upon to attempt something for which he had no training. He tried to apply modern methods to pieces which demanded insistently the fashions of an earlier time, and which lost much of their effect when they were not played in the key in which they were composed originally. To transpose them was to rob them of their special quality. And no better illustration of this could be found than the comparison of 'Fédora' as performed by Sarah-Bernhardt and by Duse. The French actress belongs to the older school; and she is mistress of all the tricks of the trade as they were practised forty and fifty years ago. 'Fédora' is a show-piece, written around the actress; it is a play full of sound and fury, signifying nothing. Her performance of the part is incomparably brilliant, a masterpiece of bravura. The Italian actress, on the other hand, tried to make the character real and poignant; and this was patently impossible. The more veracious Duse was, the more she exposed the unveracity of Sardou. But a comparison of Duse and of Sarah-Bernhardt in a more modern play — in Sudermann's 'Heimat,' for example, which we know as 'Magda' — was altogether to the advantage of the younger performer.

XVII

"THERE are gains for all our
losses," as the poet says, — even
if there are also losses for all our gains.
We lost something, no doubt, when the
old stock-companies past out of exist-
ence, — such stock-companies as the
London Haymarket, or Wallack's, or
Daly's. These companies contained
many admirable actors who were accustomed to each other, and who understood all the advantages of team-
play. But it was always a matter of
chance whether they could be fitted
into a new play. The first performance of the 'Shaughraun' at Wallack's
lingers in the memory of all who had
the good fortune to see it as the best
possible example of the work of a good

stock-company. There was Boucicault himself, in the center of the stage
all the time; there were Henry Mon-
tague and Ada Dyas as the pair of
lovers, a delight to recall; there was
Harry Beckett as the cowardly villain;
and there was John Gilbert as the
kindly priest. But there were also
two important characters intrusted to
actors entirely unsuited to them, —
good enough performers in other parts,
but hopelessly miscast in this play.
They were square pegs in round holes;
and in every performance of the good
old stock-companies the spectators
were likely to find one or more square
pegs in round holes, simply because
the manager had to do the best he
could with the performers on his salary-
list. Nowadays the effort is made to
find an actor exactly suited to the
part; and as a result the best performances of today have a harmony, a

finish, very rarely seen in the best performances of yesterday.

It is to be said also that the actors of the old stock-companies played each of them his own "line of business," as it was called; and he was very likely to play all his parts in much the same way. He did not realize that all acting ought to be character-acting. He was tempted to do his work in rough-and-ready fashion; and to repeat himself in every play in which he was called upon to appear. Perhaps Mr. George Bernard Shaw is a little over-emphatic in expressing his contempt for the laziness and the incompetence only too often seen even in fairly good companies under the old conditions. "Having been brought up on the old stock-company actor," Mr. Shaw declares, "I knew that he was the least versatile of beings, — that he was nailed helplessly to his own line of heavy or light, young or old, and played all the parts that fell to him as the representative of that line in exactly the same way. I knew that his power of hastily swallowing the words of a part and disgorging them at short notice, more or less inaccurately and quite unimprovably (three months' rehearsal would have left him more at sea than three hours'), was incompatible with his ever knowing his part in any serious sense at all."

The answer to those who assert, truthfully enough, that the older plays are not now acted as well as they used to be, is that the newer plays are acted far better than they would have been in the days of the old stock-companies. Performances like those of 'Secret Service,' of 'Arizona,' of 'Shore Acres,' of the 'Thunderbolt,' were quite impossible under the earlier conditions. To-day every play is cast to players specially engaged because they are believed to be physically or temperamentally fitted for the performance of the part intrusted to each of them. No doubt, there are failures enough today; but they are far fewer in our best theaters now than they were in the foremost playhouses of half a century ago. And I for one do not believe that the actors of our time are in any way inferior to the actors of the past, even if they do their work under different conditions. They may not succeed always when they attempt the plays of an earlier day, but their failure is not as complete as the failure of the older actors would be if it were possible to call upon them to appear in our modern realistic drama, where every part is more or less of a character-part, and where the actor, standing on a fully lighted stage, is expected to get his effect sometimes by his speech, but also often merely by a gesture or only by a look. Our actors are now less rhetorical and more pictorial, — as they must be on the picture-frame stage of our modern theater.